OLD GLORY

Part III of
Trilogy: '04-'05-'06

Brett Neveu

BROADWAY PLAY PUBLISHING INC
224 E 62nd St, NY, NY 10065
info@broadwayplaypub.com
www.broadwayplaypub.com

OLD GLORY
© Copyright 2016 by Brett Neveu

First printing: July 2016
I S B N: 978-0-88145-643-1

Book design: Marie Donovan
Typographic controls: Adobe InDesign
Typeface: Palatino
Printed and bound in the U S A

OLD GLORY premiered at Writers Theatre (Michael Halberstam, Artistic Director) in Glencoe, Illinois, running from 3 February–29 March 2009. The cast and creative contributors were:

TORLIEF.. Tom McElroy
PETER .... Phillip Earl Johnson
RAT ....Marcus Truschinski
GOSS.. Steve Haggard
MARGARET .... Penny Slusher
SCOTT... LaShawn Banks

Director..William Brown
Scenic design.. Keith Pitts
Costume design......................................Rachel Anne Healy
Lighting design ....Charles Cooper
Sound design... Andy Hansen
Properties design...Meredith Miller
Stage management .... David Castellanos

CHARACTERS & SETTING

TORLIEF, *male, Texan, Caucasian, mid-fifties*
PETER, *male, Midwestern, Caucasian, early sixties*
RAT, *male, Caucasian, twenty-four*
GOSS, *male, Caucasian, twenty-one*
MARGARET, *female, half-Puerto Rican, mid-fifties*
SCOTT, *male, Texan, African-American, twenty-six*

Place:
A bar in Berlin, Germany
A make-shift barracks in Fallujah, Iraq
A living room in a house in Mesilla, New Mexico

Time:
December 14, 2006
April 25, 2006
September 3, 2006

DEFINITIONS & TRANSLATIONS:

Einen halben Liter Pilsener, bitte: "A half-pint of pilsner, please."

Haji: anyone or anything Middle Eastern

Dank Haji or Haji Juice: Iraqi-made alcohol, usually 90 proof. Often laced with amphetamines or tranquilizers.

Amph: amphetamines

Gen. Or. 1: General order No. 1—General order that does not permit drinking or fraternizing in Iraq and Kuwait.

BDK: big, dumb kid

IED: improvised explosive device

Dismount: dismounted improvised explosive device

Rat Trap: Humvee with cobbled together armor plating

Sklid: helmet (short for "skid-lid")

Kneipen: small German bar (pronounced "Ka Nipe An")

Scene 1

(*Lights up. It is midday. An older bar in Berlin, Germany. The bar is empty, save for two men seated at a bar, their winter coats hung on hooks nearby.* PETER *wears a rumpled plaid shirt and khaki pants and* TORLIEF *wears jeans and a pressed, salmon-colored shirt.* PETER *has near him a half-filled, half-liter glass stein of beer.*)

TORLIEF: New Mexico.

PETER: Where about?

TORLIEF: Mesilla, just south of Las Cruces, north of El Paso on 10.

PETER: El Paso. I been there.

TORLIEF: Mesilla's north, north-west a bit of El Paso.

PETER: You originally from Mesilla?

TORLIEF: Nearby, but not originally.

PETER: Mesilla, New Mexico.

TORLIEF: Yeah.

PETER: I been to Albuquerque. Years ago.

TORLIEF: Santa Fe?

PETER: Nope. (*Beat*) That whole damn state is pretty.

TORLIEF: Mostly.

PETER: Scenic all the way across I bet. (*Beat*) I spent most of my time in the Cleveland area.

TORLIEF: Lake Erie.

PETER: Got your newer stadiums out there, Browns and Indians.

TORLIEF: Never been there.

PETER: This your farthest away?

TORLIEF: Yes.

PETER: Damn fine beer at a place like this. Spaten. It's fresh. It's smooth. You want one?

TORLIEF: I'm all right.

PETER: I'll get ya one, you let me know. *(Pause)* How'd you make your way to this place?

TORLIEF: Wandered, I suppose.

PETER: Wandered here?

TORLIEF: Off the beaten path.

PETER: You like doing that?

TORLIEF: Usually.

PETER: Wandering the local beer houses.

TORLIEF: Just out gettin' a sense of it.

PETER: That's how you know a place.

TORLIEF: Especially where to get a drink.

PETER: Best places to go when traveling. Food's usually the best there, too. I was once staying outside of London and the guy I was with drove he and me out to a pub in one of those dinky English countryside towns. The two of us sat in this low room at this tiny table by a big stone fireplace and he ordered for both of us and damn if that wasn't some of the best food I'd ever had. Best roast I ever tasted and the Guiness was as fresh as it could come. My god.

TORLIEF: Always wanted to go there.

PETER: England? London is pretty nice. Busy as all get out, but nice mostly. Why you in Berlin?

TORLIEF: Vacation.

PETER: Seriously? You came to Germany for vacation?

TORLIEF: I did.

PETER: In December?

TORLIEF: Yes.

PETER: You have German ancestry?

TORLIEF: Probably a little.

PETER: But no German relatives here or any of that?

TORLIEF: No.

PETER: Just came to Berlin. *(Beat)* I was in the military, stationed here for awhile after Vietnam. Just recently I retired and came back. The place somehow feels comfortable, a sorta sweet spot I guess. But I don't think I would have chose it just from pointing at a map.

TORLIEF: I'm liking it.

PETER: You been around anywhere?

TORLIEF: Not yet.

PETER: Where you staying?

TORLIEF: A place close by.

PETER: To here?

TORLIEF: No, a place close to the main area.

PETER: Touristy down there, lots of people.

TORLIEF: I haven't had a chance to check it out.

PETER: You here by yourself, then?

TORLIEF: Yeah.

PETER: Divorced?

TORLIEF: No, just away.

PETER: Left the lady at home?

TORLIEF: Yep.

PETER: Getting too much for ya, needed a break?

TORLIEF: No, just came by myself.

PETER: How long you gonna be away?

TORLIEF: Not long.

PETER: Week or so?

TORLIEF: Around that, yeah.

PETER: Let me buy you a beer.

TORLIEF: I'll have one in a bit.

PETER: Let me buy one for you now and you can wait to have it if you want.

TORLIEF: I want to just sit for a bit beforehand.

PETER: Before you have a beer?

TORLIEF: Yeah, just for a bit.

PETER: I suppose all that wandering pooped you out a little. Probably glad to sit down.

TORLIEF: I am.

PETER: Place like this doesn't usually welcome strangers very well. You should be glad you ran into me. I'll take you under my wing once the locals start to show. I'll introduce you around.

TORLIEF: Don't plan on sitting too long.

PETER: Want to keep on with your looking at the sights? This place is a heck of a sight, you should stick around.

TORLIEF: I'm only stopping in for a drink.

PETER: Which you're gonna have in a bit.

TORLIEF: Yeah.

PETER: But not now because you're resting.

TORLIEF: Yeah.

PETER: But you will soon.

TORLIEF: I will.

PETER: I can't wait.

TORLIEF: Why's that.

PETER: I think you'll like the beer. *(Pause)* Listen—
Tor—what was it again?

TORLIEF: Torlief.

PETER: What kind of name is that, anyhow?

TORLIEF: Dutch.

PETER: Dutch?

TORLIEF: Yeah.

PETER: Listen. Torlief. I think I know why you're here.
I think I know why you're talking to me. I think you
probably got a beef and you found out where I like to
come by and you have something to say.

TORLIEF: I'm not here to say anything.

PETER: I can tell by the cadence of conversation how
this thing is gonna play out.

TORLIEF: I don't have any "cadence of conversation."

PETER: You're avoidance of topics, your never-been-
anywhere-before hick-American bullshit, your lack of
a traveling companion, your desire to show up at this
bar in the early afternoon and sit with me and chat. I
been in this situation before, I been in the army most
of my life, all over the goddamn world from Vietnam
to goddamn Moscow to the fucking Sandinistas, and it
all plays the same, you got some beef, some shit with
somebody I knew or was in charge of and now you're
here to yell or poke at me so just spill and get it out and
then leave me the hell alone.

TORLIEF: It's not like that.

PETER: It *is* like that.

TORLIEF: It's not like that.

PETER: Who was it, your son?

(A pause)

TORLIEF: It was.

PETER: And what did he do?

TORLIEF: Nothing.

PETER: So what do you think I did?

TORLIEF: Nothing.

PETER: All right. Well, if you ain't gonna spill then go ahead and leave me alone.

TORLIEF: My son was Mike Hald.

PETER: Mike Hald?

TORLIEF: Yeah.

(A pause)

PETER: I should be asking you the questions.

TORLIEF: I don't have any answers.

PETER: And you think I do?

TORLIEF: I think you do, yeah.

PETER: Well. I don't.

TORLIEF: I want you to answer a few things.

PETER: I said I don't have any answers for you.

TORLIEF: I bet you do.

PETER: I've said and said to too many people lately and I got nuthin' left.

TORLIEF: Don't care.

PETER: I'm sure you don't.

TORLIEF: I don't.

PETER: Whole thing feels like a fucking echo that won't die. *(Pause)* All right. Then. If we're gonna sit, I'm buyin' you a beer.

TORLIEF: You're not going anywhere until we talk.

PETER: I know I'm not. That's why I offered you the beer. Jesus.

(A pause)

TORLIEF: All right.

PETER: Same as me?

TORLIEF: Yeah.

PETER: And we'll talk.

TORLIEF: We'll talk.

PETER: All right. *(To bartender) Einen halben Liter Pilsener, bitte.*

(Lights fade to black.)

Scene 2

(Lights up. It is early afternoon. A make-shift barracks in a crumbling Iraqi mansion. Two beds are pushed against a wall and posters, letters and other items hang nearby. RAT, *dressed in Operation Iraqi Freedom fatigues, sits on one of the beds. He reads a slim paperback titled The Big-Deal Tournament of Sub-Par Champions and Other Short Stories by Steve Starley.* GOSS, *dressed similarly to* RAT, *stands near him.)*

GOSS: Merk got his amph and that dank haji and went out in it.

RAT: Last night?

GOSS: Last night, yeah, night before.

RAT: That's nuts.

GOSS: It's not nuts, it's *right*.

RAT: How's it right?

GOSS: He goes out, down on that dank and up on the amph and crosses the threshold and bam—he's seein' things nobody else sees.

RAT: So he gets himself super-powers?

GOSS: That mix'll get you whatever you need.

RAT: Make you messed up on patrol, mostly.

GOSS: I'm saying that Merk, he can see in the dark or some shit, he can hear the flutter of a whatever, he can smell tirefire smoke burning from miles away.

RAT: His shit messed up like it is.

GOSS: It's not messed. It's attuned.

RAT: Attuned to being a messed up jackass. Fucking Gen. Or. 1, anyhow.

GOSS: Like you care about G O one.

RAT: Merk should care.

GOSS: You don't barely know Merk and you talkin' shit about him.

RAT: I know Merk well enough to know that with or without, he's a half-fucked BDK anyhow.

GOSS: BDK, yeah.

RAT: You admit it, then?

GOSS: I admit he's dumb but the shit I'm talkin' about ain't about smarts, it's about body waves, brain waves.

RAT: No matter the haji juice and amph or whatever he puts into himself, it don't make him super-human.

GOSS: Makes him something, though.

RAT: Something you think worth talking about.

GOSS: Hillson'll listen to me.

RAT: Go on over, then.

GOSS: Nah, I wanna be by my shit.

RAT: Then stop talkin' about fucking Merk.

GOSS: Merk'll get me some of that dank shit, I want it. He said the haji sold it to him promised it'd be like no other and you talk to Merk and he'll say the haji was top. *(Pause)* Back home I knew this elevator operator who'd make this moonshine that would knock your ass off. He was a hillbilly. And we used to get drinks at this one Chinese place, too.

RAT: Underage?

GOSS: Yeah.

(RAT puts his book aside.)

RAT: Me and my buddies used to go to a Chinese place, too, get drinks.

GOSS: Must be a lack there among the Chinese for cardin'.

RAT: Or just a giving spirit.

GOSS: Or a ching-chong language barrier.

(A long pause)

RAT: You hear from Becktro?

GOSS: Not since Tuesday.

RAT: What's she up to then?

GOSS: Aw, her crew's up near Baqubah.

RAT: What they got?

GOSS: Same as here—haji in the wind, settin' off the same.

RAT: You hear about Dex from 5th?

GOSS: I know Dex?

RAT: Dex, with Gidrey and Xeno?

GOSS: Aw, yeah, okay—

RAT: I E D.

GOSS: When was that?

RAT: Yesterday.

GOSS: Where he up at?

RAT: Airport.

GOSS: Anybody else?

RAT: Nobody I knew, just him.

GOSS: He hurt?

RAT: Face, arm, leg.

GOSS: Oh yeah?

RAT: Tore him up.

GOSS: Hajis, blow ya straight up.

RAT: Dex, he and me was talkin' once, he said he was up on some ridge, down some sandbox road and the sun was comin' up, he said it looked like the end of the world maybe.

GOSS: Poetic.

RAT: Or the start of the world, I forget which he said.

GOSS: Shit out there looks like both. *(Beat)* Dex say anything else?

RAT: He got to talkin' about golf.

GOSS: Golf?

RAT: He said they had a club in their rat trap, a five iron, they'd get some golf balls shipped to 'em and hit 'em out when they could. Set up a flag sometimes in the distance whereever they were and hit a bucket of balls.

GOSS: Hit a goddamn haji in the head, maybe.

RAT: Good way to check for dismounts—get out, hit a ball into it.

GOSS: Dex get back at it, he'll hit that shit again.

RAT: Yeah, soon, maybe.

GOSS: Damn that shit tear up a guy, sklid or none.

RAT: Get in your face, sometimes sklid don't matter.

GOSS: Walk out there the fuck nekkid and see what happens to ya.

RAT: Suit is the protector—we need that shit on our faces.

GOSS: You don't wanna go home with no lips?

RAT: You jokin'?

GOSS: What about no ears?

RAT: No way, that either.

GOSS: Which one would you do? Ears or lips?

RAT: Dumb ass question. Ears.

GOSS: Let your hair get long, cover 'em up.

RAT: Exactly.

GOSS: No lips, you'd be like muh muh mmmmmmmmuh.

RAT: My point.

GOSS: What about burns on your face or burns on your dick?

RAT: Nobody burnin' my dick.

GOSS: So face?

RAT: Yeah.

GOSS: But without that face, nobody gonna touch that dick.

RAT: My charm don't come from pretty, but from class and skill.

GOSS: You wish.

RAT: You'd go with burned dick?

GOSS: Yeah—then get some of that good ole' U S A reconstructive surgery and get mine all Hulkified.

RAT: What, green?

GOSS: Yeah. Green. And you wouldn't like it when it was angry.

RAT: I wouldn't like it anytime.

GOSS: You mean all the time.

RAT: That's what your moms said.

(A beat)

GOSS: Don't talk shit about my moms. She a bad-ass.

RAT: Your mom's a "bad-ass." *(Beat)* That's *great.*

(A pause)

GOSS: I'm gonna go see if I can track down Hillson.

RAT: All right, see ya.

(GOSS *begins to exit.* RAT *returns to his book.)*

GOSS: Don't touch that *Ultimate Hearthunter Collection* my bad-ass moms sent me, neither, while I'm out. I find that leather cover touched with scuff, I'll kick your ass out between tomorrow and the next.

RAT: Yeah, I'm gonna "touch" it.

GOSS: Seriously, leave it the hell alone.

RAT: Get the fuck out.

GOSS: Don't go near it. Seriously. It's my goddamn book so leave it the fuck there where it is.

(A beat)

RAT: Say "hey" to Hillson for me.

(GOSS takes off. Lights fade to black.)

Scene 3

(Lights up. A smallish living room in a townhouse in Mesilla, New Mexico. The room is furnished in a mix of bright new furniture and Southwestern knickknacks. Sitting on the couch is MARGARET, dressed in comfortable clothes. Seated next to her is SCOTT, a young man in jeans and a faded polo shirt. They each hold a can of Diet Coke.)

MARGARET: Your classes were okay?

SCOTT: They were a bit tough.

MARGARET: When do you start up again?

SCOTT: Just under a month or so.

MARGARET: And Monica is okay?

SCOTT: Getting bigger every day.

MARGARET: Sleep must be difficult for both of you.

SCOTT: Theresa's usually up first but I take over pretty quick after that. We're trying to work it on a schedule with the naps and the feedings and everything. It's tough with school and the time I want to be at home, but it'll be good once its through, then I won't have the job and school, I hopefully'll just have the job.

MARGARET: How is Theresa?

SCOTT: She's been doing some at-home stuff on the computer at night. We keep sayin' that it'd be nice to spend more time together but the whole thing's a means to an end, that once Monica's older and I get through everything, we'll come out the other side and it'll all settle down.

MARGARET: You need a good perspective.

SCOTT: Yes ma'am.

MARGARET: But be careful of over-practicality.

SCOTT: Right. *(Pause)* How long since Torlief went back to work?

MARGARET: Early August. Steve Mackon's been helpful, letting him off some at the beginning.

SCOTT: Torlief at work now?

MARGARET: He went on some calls this morning but he'll be back soon.

(A beat)

SCOTT: What have you been up to? Your sister's still coming in?

MARGARET: She and I go out to the swap meet south of town every once in awhile.

SCOTT: That's good.

MARGARET: Just to look around. *(Pause)* This is just a quick visit?

SCOTT: I wanted to stop by to say hello.

MARGARET: You should have called first and let me know you were coming. I could have had lunch ready.

SCOTT: I sort of just came on a whim.

(A pause)

MARGARET: Have you heard from Jamie?

SCOTT: No, ma'am. *(Pause)* How's Lisa doing in school?

MARGARET: Her junior year just started about a month ago. Seems like she's trying to play catch-up still a bit.

SCOTT: You talk to Ben Axman?

MARGARET: Ben? No, not since the service.

SCOTT: He's headin' back.

MARGARET: He is?

SCOTT: He was recalled a few days ago.

MARGARET: That was fast. *(Beat)* What about you?

SCOTT: Haven't heard yet, but it's a strong possibility. *(A pause)* Where's Torlief out at?

MARGARET: He's not to far, just northwest.

SCOTT: Almagordo?

MARGARET: Around there.

SCOTT: So not far.

MARGARET: Just an hour away from here, pretty much.

SCOTT: I have a cousin near Almagordo. Marty. He doesn't do much of anything but sit on his behind, stuff chew in his lip and watch satellite T V. *(Pause)* You all haven't gotten any recent calls from army folks, have ya?

MARGARET: Calls from army folks?

SCOTT: Yes, ma'am.

MARGARET: Why, is the army trying to call me?

SCOTT: If you haven't, then no.

MARGARET: Why are you asking me that?

SCOTT: I just heard a few things.

MARGARET: Who would be trying to call me?

SCOTT: Someone regarding Mike, maybe.

MARGARET: Someone is supposed to call here?

SCOTT: I'm not sure.

MARGARET: Why would somebody call?

SCOTT: What time's Torlief back?

MARGARET: Should be around five.

(A pause)

SCOTT: Can I get another Diet Coke?

MARGARET: Another?

SCOTT: If that's all right.

MARGARET: Yeah. Go on and help yourself.

(A beat. SCOTT stands.)

SCOTT: In the fridge?

MARGARET: In the garage.

SCOTT: The garage?

MARGARET: That way.

(MARGARET points.)

SCOTT: Where in the garage?

MARGARET: In the fridge in the garage. By the door.

SCOTT: Okay.

MARGARET: Jesus. Just—go right in there. Right there.

(MARGARET points again. SCOTT exits toward the garage.)

(Lights fade to black.)

Scene 4

(Lights up on PETER and TORLIEF at the German bar. Both have half-filled steins of beer before them.)

PETER: It was a bad rebound thing, anyhow.

TORLIEF: You were in charge.

PETER: I was never in exact direct charge.

TORLIEF: They were your orders.

PETER: The orders to me were to follow procedure.

TORLIEF: Keeping it like that.

PETER: It was a complicated situation.

TORLIEF: Lies.

PETER: I'm not lying.

TORLIEF: There were lies.

PETER: Nope.

TORLIEF: Again and again.

PETER: It wasn't lies.

TORLIEF: You're lying right now.

PETER: Nope.

TORLIEF: The kid shot and murdered him.

PETER: Sorry, old news.

TORLIEF: Jesus.

PETER: Bein' blunt.

TORLIEF: Lies lies lies.

PETER: They've worked it out now, that boy's under lock and key, he ain't gonna go nowhere no more.

TORLIEF: For ten months.

PETER: Twelve months.

TORLIEF: Maximum, twelve months.

PETER: Maximum, twelve months.

TORLIEF: Why was his dishonorable discharge reduced?

PETER: You'd have to talk to—

TORLIEF:—you, I'm talking to you.

PETER: A bad conduct discharge is no slap on the wrist.

TORLIEF: But you knew the truth!

PETER: And now so do you.

TORLIEF: It doesn't balance out!

PETER: You need to stop yelling or we'll both be out of this place right on our asses.

(*A pause*)

TORLIEF: You knew what he was doing.

PETER: Kid wasn't up to nuthin' 'cept being a dumb-ass recruit.

TORLIEF: Unsafe handling—

PETER: Previous reports of unsafe handling of his firearm, yeah.

TORLIEF: Yes.

PETER: I don't deny it.

TORLIEF: Your responsibility to keep in check.

PETER: Babysitting wasn't my responsibility in Fallujah. The I E Ds were my responsibility. The ambushes. The night patrols. I had my responsibilities and you weren't the fuck there so stop armchair quarterbackin' my time.

TORLIEF: You feel guilt over this.

PETER: I don't.

TORLIEF: You feel guilt.

PETER: It's not that dramatic.

TORLIEF: I can feel the guilt off of you.

PETER: You can't.

(PETER *takes a sip of his beer.*)

TORLIEF: You're gonna come back with me.

PETER: Come back where?

TORLIEF: Back with me home to New Mexico.

PETER: I am?

TORLIEF: Yeah.

PETER: To do what?

TORLIEF: Talk to my wife.

PETER: To who?

TORLIEF: To my wife. And to the army.

PETER: I'm gonna talk?

TORLIEF: Yeah.

PETER: What for?

TORLIEF: You're just gonna do it.

PETER: That's stupid.

TORLIEF: It's what you're gonna do.

PETER: What am I supposed to say?

TORLIEF: You're gonna tell my wife the truth.

PETER: You know the truth.

TORLIEF: You're gonna tell the army what happened!

PETER: Relax with me for a minute.

TORLIEF: No—

PETER: Relax.

TORLIEF: No—

PETER: Let's finish our beers and relax.

TORLIEF: No!

PETER: Let's sit here and relax for a minute.

TORLIEF: You and me are going to New Mexico.

PETER: Whatever you want me to do or whatever you want me to say ain't goin' nowhere right now so sit here with me for a minute. Just do that. *(Pause)* What do you do back in New Mexico? *(Pause)* What do you do back home?

(A long pause)

TORLIEF: I sell feed additives for cattle.

PETER: Feed additives?

TORLIEF: Antibiotics, hormones, that sort of thing.

PETER: From a store?

TORLIEF: I'm a rep.

PETER: Like a drug rep?

TORLIEF: Yeah.

PETER: For cows?

TORLIEF: Yeah.

PETER: Who do you call on, veterinarians?

TORLIEF: Yeah, them and ranchers.

PETER: So a lot of driving?

TORLIEF: Yes.

PETER: You have any head yourself?

TORLIEF: No.

PETER: Keep any animals?

(A beat)

TORLIEF: Two horses.

PETER: Oh yeah? What kind?

TORLIEF: Two-year-old black and white tobiano filly and a seven year old paint gelding.

PETER: When I was a boy this uncle of mine had a paint gelding.

TORLIEF: Good horse around kids.

PETER: Gelding's name was Slim Tim.

TORLIEF: Ours are Summer and RedRock.

PETER: RedRock. That Mike's horse?

TORLIEF: Yeah.

PETER: And the other—

TORLIEF: My daughter's.

PETER: You live on a big parcel of land?

TORLIEF: We're out on the edge of town a bit, plenty of places to ride.

PETER: Where did Mike usually take Red?

TORLIEF: There's a table rock not far, he used to like going up there.

PETER: Sounds good. *(Beat)* My uncle who had that paint gelding, he was in a wheelchair. He'd push that thing right out to the fence, lean on the barbs and Slim Tim would come right over and he'd sit there and feed him. I remember thinking that the horse might chew his knee off, him with his knees stickin' out from that wheelchair, that the horse might get mistaken and bite his knee.

(A pause)

TORLIEF: Mike liked taking Red out real early in the morning.

PETER: I bet it's like a movie at your place when the sun comes up.

TORLIEF: That's what he'd do, Mike'd ride out in the morning and watch the sun, hit a few trails then head on back in time for school.

PETER: My uncle who had that paint gelding, he made me stand on it once. He said "Get up there and stand on him and see what he does."

TORLIEF: Was he barebacked?

PETER: Yeah.

TORLIEF: You do it?

PETER: I trusted my uncle. And the horse. But I do remember after I was standing there, Slim Tim shifting under me, I thought, "How did my uncle get in that wheelchair, anyway?"

TORLIEF: From standing on a horse?

PETER: Nope. Childhood polio.

(TORLIEF *and* PETER *laugh lightly.* PETER *pokes at* TORLIEF'*s beer.*)

PETER: You need to have another.

TORLIEF: I don't think so.

PETER: You shouldn't squander your time at a great Kneipen like we got here. One more Spaten.

TORLIEF: No.

PETER: How much longer you in Berlin?

TORLIEF: Three more days.

PETER: But maybe earlier you get me out of this bar and drag me off to New Mexico so I can tell my truth to everybody. (*Pause*) I'm gettin' us more Spaten.

(*A long pause*)

TORLIEF: Fine.

PETER: Good.

TORLIEF: All right.

PETER: Good.

(*Lights fade to black.*)

Scene 5

(*Lights up on the make-shift barracks.* GOSS *and* RAT *sit on their bunks,* GOSS *reading his* Hearthunter *anthology comic and* RAT *reading his book of short stories.* GOSS *is a bit drunk.*)

GOSS: You ever read Hearthunter?

RAT: No.

GOSS: You should sometime.

RAT: I'm reading this here.

GOSS: You should get some, just sometime, and read it. Bet you'd like it.

RAT: Doubt that.

GOSS: In this one, in this one I'm reading—The Hearthunter's trapped in the middle of what was New York City and the Revelers are comin', they got a soldier in every rubble pile and then Legion Killer is in hot pursuit, too, so it's gonna be a battle between Legion, the Revelers and The Hearthunter—and on toppa that, The Hearthunter's poisoned, he got poisoned by some bad water.

RAT: Bad water?

GOSS: He drank some bad water and it's killing him real slow.

RAT: This guy's like a super hero and he's maybe gonna die from some bad water?

GOSS: The Hearthunter ain't a super hero. He caught a virus that deformed him and made him an adrenaline junkie, makes him eat human hearts to stay alive. And the goddamn world was torn apart by the same virus epidemic, so poisons are everywhere, especially in the water.

RAT: Then why did he drink it?

GOSS: He thought it was fine.

RAT: Why did he think it was fine?

GOSS: It tested fine.

RAT: So he tests all water before he drinks it?

GOSS: He'd have to or he'd be poisoned.

RAT: Why didn't he catch the poison with his test?

GOSS: I'm not explainin' all this.

RAT: I'm just curious.

Goss: Then read it.

Rat: I'm curious about the logic.

Goss: I'm not explainin' the logic. Read it if you wanna know.

Rat: I don't wanna read it. I only want you to tell me why the logic is warped.

Goss: The logic ain't warped!

Rat: Sounds warped.

Goss: Only cuz you don't know the background!

Rat: Probably muddle it even more.

Goss: It ain't muddled, it's complicated. It's all really complicated. Especially in the earlier issues from back in the mid-nineties. There's all sorts of background info, things that come up, things that The Hearthunter, he thinks about, things from the past.

Rat: Truly incredible stuff, Gossimer.

Goss: It is.

Rat: Brainfood.

Goss: Stop fuckin' with me, okay, Rat?

Rat: No, seriously, I think you're a damn lit-buff. Put on your glasses and turn on the CSPAN, time to navigate a wordy passage or two.

Goss: This shit's a graphic novel. *Novel.* Graphic Novel.

Rat: I get it, sweetheart.

Goss: You're not the keen shit you think you are, Rat-o.

Rat: I'm no keen shit.

Goss: Naw, you think you're keen shit. You think you got stuff figured, it's all cool for Ratty.

Rat: You're the one who started talkin' about your comic book.

GOSS: It's not a goddamn comic book!

RAT: You're the one who started talkin'.

GOSS: Hearthunter's some inspiring shit is all and I thought maybe you'd wanna check it.

RAT: Demented shit, what it is.

GOSS: And you don't read demented shit?

RAT: I don't.

GOSS: You don't like demented movies?

RAT: Good plot, demented or whatever, fine by me.

GOSS: That's what I'm sayin'. Hearthunter's got a good plot.

RAT: How's the writing?

GOSS: It's good, too. Scotty Gerome wrote this issue.

RAT: Scotty Gerome.

GOSS: Guy that did that show, *Triland Empire*.

RAT: Jesus.

GOSS: Why don't you go on someplace else you got nuthin' but shit to say.

RAT: You go someplace else.

GOSS: Go wander before patrol.

RAT: *You* go wander before patrol.

GOSS: Nobody asked you to have opinions about my shit!

RAT: You're the one askin' me questions about your damn comic book.

GOSS: GRAPHIC NOVEL!

RAT: See this? *(Holds up book) This* is a novel.

GOSS: No it ain't. That's a book of short stories.

RAT: Steve Starley's a great novelist, too, that's my fucking point.

(A beat)

GOSS: You think I'm some kind of dipshit, dontcha?

RAT: Not especially.

GOSS: You askin' for somethin' from me?

RAT: What would I be askin' from you?

GOSS: You want some shit from me?

RAT: What would I want?

GOSS: You want me to come at you or what?

RAT: What?

GOSS: You want it and I'll come at you over this shit.

RAT: I don't want nuthin' except to lie here and read my goddamn book.

GOSS: That ain't gonna happen. You opened up this can and it ain't goin' back in.

RAT: Why don't you take your own advice and wander before patrol.

GOSS: The stuff that's shit is the stuff you're readin'.

RAT: You're entitled to your opinion.

GOSS: You think sayin' somethin' like that makes it better?

RAT: Drop it.

GOSS: What you said about my shit and me goes deeper than opinion.

RAT: You want me to say "sorry?"

GOSS: Hell no!

RAT: Sorry.

GOSS: I don't want your "sorry!" What I want is respect.

RAT: For what?

GOSS: For the kinda shit I do.

RAT: Your head's up your ass.

GOSS: That ain't the kind of respectful statement I was looking for.

RAT: Just cuz I don't like somethin' of yours don't mean you gotta take it personal.

GOSS: But I do.

RAT: But you don't have to.

GOSS: So I choose to.

RAT: What for?

GOSS: Cuz of you. Sayin' things that you say. Lookin' at me that way and shit.

RAT: What in the hell does that even mean?

GOSS: This some deep shit, Ritty-Rat. You don't wanna play with shit this deep.

RAT: I don't wanna hear about shit this deep.

GOSS: And that's the deal—you all don't care.

RAT: Me all?

GOSS: You look the fuck right through.

RAT: Yeah?

GOSS: What you doin' over here, anyhow? A person like you, sittin' like you do, you got plenty places to be and here you sit and when you sit you look at everybody like you own France or some shit. You think you smell like front-lawn flowers but in the end you there on the floor, you there on the road, you there with dust in your shit just like every single one of everybody else. You look at me like my shit ain't

here, but know this: my shit's here and it ain't gonna
do nuthin' but blow the fuck up in your face, ker-boom
bam ker-blast.

(A beat)

RAT: I don't want this conversation.

GOSS: Cuz you know the shit I speak.

RAT: Calm the fuck down and read your fucking book.

GOSS: My book?

RAT: Yeah. Your book.

GOSS: You sayin' this is a book, now?

RAT: If it gets you down to read it, yeah, it's a book.

(GOSS grabs his pistol.)

GOSS: Don't patronize me, motherfucker. I'll kill ya in
your sleep.

RAT: C'mon. Gossamer. Sit down and read.

GOSS: I'll sit and read when I sit and read. You sit and
read! Jerkoff.

*(A pause. GOSS puts his pistol away. RAT opens his book
and reads. GOSS slides down to his bunk and opens his book.)*

RAT: What're ya drinkin', anyhow?

GOSS: Jack.

RAT: You wanna give me a bit?

GOSS: Yeah, all right.

*(GOSS hands RAT a small bottle of Jack Daniels. RAT takes a
long swig, then hands it back to GOSS.)*

RAT: Thanks.

GOSS: Jerkoff.

*(A pause. Somewhere nearby hip-hop music begins to play.
A pause. GOSS picks up his rifle and begins to exit toward
the music.)*

GOSS: Yo, Yertle! Crank that beat!

(GOSS *exits. After a few moments,* RAT *follows. Lights fade to black.*)

Scene 6

(*Lights up on the living room in Mesilla, New Mexico.* SCOTT *and* MARGARET *continue to sit, each with a new Diet Coke.* MARGARET *stares off into space as* SCOTT *takes a sip of his soda.*)

SCOTT: Jamie's in Korea.

MARGARET: Jamie's in Korea? Why?

SCOTT: He's being held in protective custody.

MARGARET: But—

SCOTT: But he wasn't before.

MARGARET: I thought he was only held for awhile while they talked to him and then he was put back on active duty in Iraq.

SCOTT: He was sent to Korea.

MARGARET: Why was Jamie sent to Korea?

SCOTT: He was reassigned.

MARGARET: Reassigned?

SCOTT: They stationed him there and then something happened and he went AWOL but then later they found him and brought him in.

MARGARET: Why did he go AWOL?

SCOTT: Problems.

MARGARET: What problems?

SCOTT: There were problems, and after they found him, Jamie gave contradictory accounts about what happened.

MARGARET: They told us the investigation was closed because they concluded what happened was an accident.

SCOTT: Jamie gave them a contradictory account from what he said before, he told them he wanted to tell them the truth.

MARGARET: What did he say, what did Jamie say he was doing if he wasn't loading his gun?

SCOTT: What I'd thought happened. That Mike's death wasn't an accident. *(Beat)* I'm real sorry, Margaret. I'm sorry to you and Mike and Tor. I assumed they had it and I thought they'd then tell you right off but then they shipped Jamie off to Korea and then with me now back here with the baby and everything, I didn't know what to do when. I figured the army would investigate more and let you know soon enough.

MARGARET: No one has called us about any of this.

SCOTT: I know—

MARGARET: You and me have spoken a number of times.

SCOTT: Yes, ma'am.

MARGARET: You were Mike's best friend, you should have told us if you thought what happened wasn't an accident.

SCOTT: I figured it would be their place to tell you if it was and I thought with this they would soon enough, so I'm sure they'll call.

MARGARET: We'll be calling them before they call us, I'm sure.

SCOTT: I don't doubt it.

MARGARET: We'll be calling them. *(Beat)* You should have told us. *(Pause)* Tell me how it happened.

SCOTT: I don't know exactly what went on.

MARGARET: It wasn't an accident, so what did Jamie do?

SCOTT: I can only guess.

MARGARET: Then guess.

SCOTT: He was probably messing around.

MARGARET: With his gun?

SCOTT: Doing dumb stuff, yeah. I'd seen it before. Pointing his gun, arguing, fighting. They were both drinking. Because of General Order One, there'd been a big crackdown but folks could still get whatever they wanted if they wanted to—whiskey and beer plus Haji juice—

MARGARET: Haji juice?

SCOTT: Iraqi-made liquor sometimes laced with amphetamines or maybe tranquilizers.

MARGARET: How often were Mike and Jamie drinking Haji juice?

SCOTT: Not often—

MARGARET: And everybody knew?

SCOTT: No—

MARGARET: Did Colonel Rasmussen know?

SCOTT: I don't think he knew either of them much, really.

MARGARET: He knew they argued, that they fought—

SCOTT: I don't think—

MARGARET: Did you tell him they were fighting?

SCOTT: I was asked questions—

MARGARET: So the army knew Mike's death wasn't an accident.

SCOTT: Not exactly—

MARGARET: They knew.

SCOTT: Maybe, maybe not, but Jamie's confessed to it now.

(A pause)

MARGARET: Did you see Mike after he was killed?

SCOTT: It happened right close by to where I was, so yes, ma'am, I saw him.

MARGARET: You never told me you saw him. *(Beat)* What did you see?

SCOTT: I saw Mike.

MARGARET: Where was he?

SCOTT: He was backwards on the floor. He'd been shot.

MARGARET: In the chest.

SCOTT: In the chest, yes, ma'am.

MARGARET: Where was Jamie?

SCOTT: They'd by then taken him someplace, I'm not sure where.

(A pause)

MARGARET: You been to my home a number of times.

SCOTT: Yes, ma'am.

MARGARET: I met your wife and baby daughter.

SCOTT: Yes, ma'am.

MARGARET: You looked me in the eye.

SCOTT: With all this I wanted you all to hear what was up now from me first and hopefully not before from some stranger on the phone.

MARGARET: You are a stranger.

SCOTT: I'm not. I was Mike's friend.

MARGARET: No you're not.

SCOTT: I was Mike's best friend over there.

MARGARET: I don't think you were.

SCOTT: I should go. *(He stands to exit.)*

MARGARET: Hold on.

SCOTT: I don't want to bother you further.

MARGARET: Sit down.

SCOTT: I should go.

MARGARET: Sit down.

(A beat)

SCOTT: all right. *(He sits.)*

MARGARET: I need to call Torlief. And you're going to sit there. You'll leave when I tell you to leave. I want you sit there, you goddamn son-of-a-bitch.

(A pause)

(Lights fade to black.)

Scene 7

(Lights up on the barracks. It is night. A pause. GOSS and RAT, in full patrol gear, enter.)

GOSS: It's there, jesus.

RAT: Get it, then.

(RAT begins removing some of his gear.)

GOSS: Keep your shit together, I got it. *(He looks under his bunk. He pulls out a package wrapped in a dark cloth.)* See?

RAT: Hold on—

GOSS: Yeah, all right.

(Goss places the package on his bunk and starts to remove some of his gear, also. A long pause.)

RAT: You hear her? That little girl there in the shadow, drippin' nearly on my boot.

GOSS: You sure that was her blood?

RAT: From that cut up on her forehead.

GOSS: Coulda been from either the other ones.

RAT: Why you wanna question me?

GOSS: They dragged her outa that shit, stood her up, coulda been either her's or their's.

RAT: It was her blood, so shut the fuck up.

(Goss begins to unwrap the cloth on the package.)

GOSS: Here we go.

RAT: Shit better not be poison.

GOSS: It's not poison.

RAT: That shit better not make me ill.

GOSS: Bro shutup unless you don't want none.

(Goss produces a bottle of clear liquid from the cloth wrapping.)

RAT: Pour it in some cups.

(A beat. Goss grabs two metal cups from a bin on the floor, opens the bottle and pours some of the liquid into each cup. He hands one of the cups to RAT, then hides the bottle in the bin. Goss and RAT drink from the cups, wincing as they do.)

RAT: Tastes like poison.

GOSS: Just strong is all.

RAT: Burns.

GOSS: Puss.

RAT: Goddamn.

(A pause)

GOSS: You talk to Zelda?

RAT: Yeah. He told me that they came up and wouldn't stop, so they went ahead.

GOSS: He said they warned 'em but they kept coming.

RAT: You talk to him, too?

GOSS: Yeah.

RAT: Why you askin' if I talked to him, then?

GOSS: Just wonderin' what he said to you and it maybe bein' different than what he said to me.

RAT: Why?

GOSS: Because, I don't know. *(Pause)* Zel said there was no way to see inside right, anyhow, the thing speedin' at him like that. There was no way to tell.

RAT: Soulda hit the tires, stopped it cold.

GOSS: It was movin' too fast, plus if the car's holdin' then you risk the thing goin' up. Better to stop it before it can go.

RAT: Stop it by blowing it up?

GOSS: They didn't know it would go. All they saw was a car coming.

RAT: Damn haji in the car, his kids like that, what was that about?

GOSS: I'm no goddamn mind reader.

(The power in the barracks suddenly goes out.)

GOSS: Shit.

RAT: Fuck, great.

GOSS: Damn power shit.

RAT: Fuck.

(A pause)

Goss: Maybe that little girl'll say somethin', let 'em know why they sped up. Sure as she don't know or speak English enough to say. Maybe they'll get Randy to talk to her, translate and see. They pull Randy, I bet, they'll hear what the girl knows. But the shit still went down, right, so either way, the shit's already done, her words or no words. *(Pause)* Who's 101st talkin' to? Rasmussen, probably. He'll get the best of what he can, I guess.

RAT: He'll put forth as much effort as he feels toward any sorta dead hajis.

Goss: It's serious shit, Rat. He'll do his job.

RAT: Dead haji's all over, he can't be there with every one of 'em sayin' this or that's why they're dead.

Goss: No, but he can see what the hell all took place.

RAT: You know what took place.

Goss: Do I?

RAT: Zel said and you saw after.

Goss: Yeah.

RAT: And you know the situation.

Goss: Yeah.

RAT: Then think hard on the shit again before you get too stupid.

Goss: Kiss my ass, you're the one who's stupid.

(A pause)

RAT: Pour some more juice and just fuck it.

(A pause. Goss crosses to the bin and pulls out the bottle. He pours more of the clear liquid into the two cups, then returns the bottle to the bin.)

RAT: Goddamn night patrol.

Goss: That sorta shit don't happen every time.

RAT: Some sorta shit happens.

GOSS: Then shut your eyes next time, shut your ears.

RAT: Funny.

GOSS: Cry into your cap.

(RAT *lies on his bunk. A long pause.*)

GOSS: Forget your troubles. C'mon get happy, gonna chase all your blues away. *(Sings)* Say hallelujah c'mon get happy—

(GOSS *continues singing, the song running a few times through, then ramping wildly until he's doing a full routine.* RAT, *laughing, joins in as the routine winds up.*)

GOSS & RAT: —get ready for the judgement day!

(GOSS *and* RAT *laugh.*)

GOSS: Maybe it ain't judgement day that'll come. Maybe it'll be judgement night.

RAT: That'd be somethin'. Jesus comin' for ya at night, like all the rest of the ghosts.

GOSS: Yeah, you'd be sleepin' and you'd suddenly feel a presence in the room—

RAT: "Mhuhhhhhh!"

GOSS: "What was that sound? What was that noise?"

(RAT *puts a towel over his head and raises his rifle above his arms.*)

RAT: *(Lower voice)* "Why, it's me! The ghost of Jesus Christ."

GOSS: "What the!"

RAT: "I'm totally here to haunt your house."

GOSS: "Yikes! I'm a-scared of g-g-g-g-hosts!"

RAT: "Boo boo boo boo boo."

GOSS: You'd have to have an exorcism or somethin'.

(RAT *playfullly points his rifle at* GOSS.)

RAT: But Jesus wouldn't leave with an exorcism. Probably view it like you was a big fan, bringin' in some further supporters of his work.

(GOSS *and* RAT *laugh. The laughter quiets.* RAT *puts the rifle and towel away. A long pause as* RAT *and* GOSS *share more haji juice.*)

RAT: Zel tell you how many for sure there were in the car?

(*A beat*)

GOSS: He said five hajis, maybe six.

RAT: Three kids in the back?

GOSS: Countin' the little girl, yeah, three kids.

RAT: You see the other ones?

GOSS: No, just the sheets by the road.

RAT: You see the man?

GOSS: Burnt up, still in the car, yeah.

RAT: Little girl saw it, too.

GOSS: Depressing.

RAT: No kiddin', dipshit.

GOSS: What the fuck?

RAT: "Depressing"?

GOSS: Fuck off.

RAT: Stop talkin' such obvious shit.

GOSS: So it's not depressing?

RAT: Nail on the head four thousand times.

GOSS: I'll nail you on the head four million times.

RAT: No more talk about tonight.

GOSS: What?

RAT: Starting right now there's moratorium on you talkin' about what happened.

GOSS: I talk about what I wanna talk about whenever I wanna talk, tonight or otherwise.

RAT: I don't wanna hear what you hafta say.

GOSS: Fuck that.

RAT: Stop talking.

GOSS: I talk about whatever if I want.

RAT: Better not.

(A beat)

GOSS: Exploded car. Wounded child. Dead family.

(A pause. Lights fade to black.)

Scene 8

(Lights up on the townhouse. MARGARET and SCOTT sit on the couch. MARGARET's hands are in her lap. In her right hand is a black cordless telephone. A pause. MARGARET puts the telephone down on the coffee table.)

MARGARET: Torlief and Mike argued a lot.

SCOTT: Mike told me they did, yes, ma'am.

MARGARET: Torlief didn't want him there.

SCOTT: He said.

MARGARET: Mike told you that.

SCOTT: Once, we were talking and Mike said something about how his dad felt.

MARGARET: Torlief told him it would be like that.

SCOTT: Mike knew what it could be like. You don't join up not exactly knowing.

MARGARET: He didn't know first person.

SCOTT: You don't fully know until you're there, no.
It can be chaos sometimes. And other times nothing.
Sometimes it'd get so boring I'd sit and compose e-mail
messages, I'd write 'em down longhand and type 'em
out and send 'em later.

MARGARET: What did Mike do when there was
nothing?

SCOTT: He'd sit, pass the time, come by where I was,
hang out. When he was on patrol, he was fine. He liked
activity, I think, but he didn't mind just hanging out,
too.

(A pause)

MARGARET: Is your baby doing anything new?

SCOTT: Not really.

MARGARET: I know she must be.

SCOTT: She's not old enough really to be doing much.

MARGARET: I doubt that's true.

SCOTT: Nothing impressive, at least.

MARGARET: Tell me what she's been doing.

(A pause)

SCOTT: She screams and I put her head under my chin
and hold her entire body down just to try and keep her
from losing it completely.

MARGARET: She's very young.

SCOTT: I'm doing that sometimes at four in the morning
and then sometimes in the middle of the day.

MARGARET: What else?

SCOTT: What else?

MARGARET: What else?

SCOTT: Let's see. She grabs my finger. She likes to look
at my face. She's sleeping in her crib already. It seems

weird already that before she was sleeping in a little bouncy chair at the foot of the bed.

MARGARET: Yes.

SCOTT: I figured since she was lying there next to me inside Theresa for all that time that I wouldn't notice her that much once she was in the room, but once she was there I found that I could barely sleep just knowing that was her breathin' down there.

MARGARET: What did she sound like when she slept?

SCOTT: Just breathing sounds.

MARGARET: What sounds?

SCOTT: Ahhh and oooooo sometimes.

MARGARET: Ip ip ip sometimes?

SCOTT: No, but like a chicken sometimes.

MARGARET: Bock bock bock?

SCOTT: I guess more like a turkey.

MARGARET: Gobble gobble like a turkey.

SCOTT: I imagine.

MARGARET: You imagine.

SCOTT: Bwobble, bwobble, like that.

MARGARET: Mike would get the hiccups in his sleep.

SCOTT: Moni gets like that, too, but when she's awake, hic hic hic.

MARGARET: I'd hear these little pops coming out of Mike like a metrotome, pop pop pop. My mother said I should ask the doctor if the hiccups were a problem.

SCOTT: Theresa asked.

MARGARET: So did I.

SCOTT: They're not a problem.

MARGARET: No.

SCOTT: She felt like an idiot asking.

MARGARET: So did I. But you have to ask. You need to know. And even when you know you still wonder.

(*A pause*)

SCOTT: Maybe you should try to call Torlief now.

(*A pause*)

MARGARET: When you're finished with school, where are you going to live?

SCOTT: Depends on what the army does and where I can find work. I'm not wanting to get too far away.

MARGARET: Where are you looking?

SCOTT: Maybe Austin or Santa Fe.

MARGARET: You're making some difficult decisions.

SCOTT: Getting through school will be the difficult thing. I still am not sure exactly why I picked pediatric respiratory therapy.

MARGARET: It does seem like a very difficult subject.

SCOTT: It's not all that bad, I'm getting through.

MARGARET: It sounds like if you had a job like that and you made a mistake then you could put a child's life in danger.

SCOTT: Not really.

MARGARET: Yes. Really.

SCOTT: It's a slow process for the child, respiratory therapy.

MARGARET: A possible lingering death for the child, then, is possible, from a half-hearted decision made by you. You could stop a little life even before it had a chance to begin. You would be remembered forever by that mother as the man who killed her child.

(*A pause*)

SCOTT: I should get home.

MARGARET: Don't go.

SCOTT: I should.

(MARGARET *reaches for the telephone.*)

MARGARET: I'll call Torlief now.

SCOTT: That's fine.

MARGARET: Are you hungry? (*Beat*) I'll fix you something to eat.

SCOTT: I'm not hungry.

MARGARET: I'm fixing you something and I'm fixing myself something.

SCOTT: Margaret—

MARGARET: I'll go into the kitchen. I'll fix us something. Sandwiches or there's some salad leftover. I'll go fix something for us. In a moment. We'll have something to eat. In a moment. In a moment.

(*A long pause. The two sit very still. Lights fade to black.*)

Scene 9

(*Lights up on the bar in Berlin.* TORLIEF *and* PETER *sit at the bar. They are fairly inebriated.*)

PETER: ...and she says, "Into the trash it goes".

TORLIEF: No shit?

PETER: Never did you see a grown man want to both kill and cry at the same time.

TORLIEF: Then what?

PETER: Off it went the next day.

TORLIEF: Seven years?

PETER: Was a hell of a fish.

TORLIEF: You imagine bein' your wife, openin' the freezer every time for something and seein' a three foot Northern Pike in there starin' at ya?

PETER: Gave her the creeps the moment I brought it in.

TORLIEF: Probably one of the main reasons you hung onto it so long.

PETER: *A* reason but not the main reason.

TORLIEF: Hell, that's something I woulda thought to do if my wife had complained about a fish I caught.

PETER: Hell of a struggle, when it was caught. It gave me a long fight and everybody saw.

TORLIEF: Who?

PETER: My brothers. They sat there while it went on, they sat there equally cheering and fuming, same as I woulda done had it been one of them. Saw that animal cut through the water, saw it pull, saw it chompin' the steel leader.

TORLIEF: What'd your brothers say when it was all through?

PETER: Nothing. They just casted out and tried to see if they could get the damn thing's daddy.

TORLIEF: So you froze it.

PETER: Like a sonofabitch. I'd bring it out every Thanksgiving with the turkey just to stick it their faces and shit. *(Pause)* I mostly, though, kept it because of its eyes.

TORLIEF: It's eyes?

PETER: Yeah.

TORLIEF: What?

PETER: Shit.

TORLIEF: What?

PETER: Forget it. *(Beat)* It had eyes. *(Pause)* When
the damn thing was in the water fighting I'd catch
it looking at me like it knew something about me.
It stared right into me. Like it knew something was
coming up, something that I didn't know. The fish
knew it was caught, that I had it, but I think it also
wanted me to know it had me, too, that destiny or
somethin' had brought us two together, that the fish
and me were somehow made to meet, that I knew
something about it and it knew something about me.
(Beat) Retarded, right?

TORLIEF: Justa fish.

PETER: Yeah, that's what I want to say. But I really
know the truth. That pike's eyes said dig in. It dug
far in and it knew secrets about me. My secrets. Scary
secrets. Over all my years, over all my life.

TORLIEF: Secrets like what?

PETER: That was between that fish and me.

TORLIEF: You can tell me if you want.

PETER: *(Sudden anger)* It was between that fish and me!

(A pause)

TORLIEF: But you let your wife toss it?

PETER: My wife and me both knew she coulda threw it
out anytime when I was overseas, but she didn't. She
left it to me. And I didn't do it. So eventually she did.

TORLIEF: She here with you in Berlin?

PETER: She and me not too long ago separated after
thirty years of marriage.

TORLIEF: Wow. Sorry.

PETER: Earth still turns. But shit do happen, don't it?
(Pause) I saw your boy. Afterwards, I saw him, after
he was shot. I got a look at him. I uncovered the sheet

that was over the top of him, I looked at him, smelled the alcohol on him, saw his eyes, still a bit wild even as he lay there, stiff and bloody. My heart went out. It did, went right out. My heart went out, seein' him on the floor like that. *(Pause)* I got three kids, all girls. You want onea them to make up?

TORLIEF: What?

PETER: I got one in the navy, a lawyer. They send her out same as the soldiers, send her to places all over the goddamn world, sent her to Africa just a few months ago, and then to China after that. You can have that one.

TORLIEF: I don't want your daughter.

PETER: Even trade.

TORLIEF: No.

PETER: I'm serious.

TORLIEF: No.

PETER: Fine, but remember I offered.

TORLIEF: That's awful.

PETER: I'm awful.

TORLIEF: What you said, trading your daughter, that's awful.

PETER: I'm awful. I'm awful.

(A pause)

TORLIEF: I want to go home.

PETER: You do?

TORLIEF: I want to go home.

(TORLIEF stands to leave.)

PETER: Where's your hotel?

TORLIEF: No, home-home.

PETER: Home-home?

TORLIEF: I want to go home.

PETER: You still want me to come, too?

(A pause)

TORLIEF: No.

PETER: You don't want me to come?

TORLIEF: No.

PETER: Why not?

TORLIEF: I don't wanna be here with you.

PETER: You don't?

TORLIEF: I don't wanna be here with you.

PETER: It's because we know now, is it? We know now what's inside. I see in you. You see in me.

TORLIEF: I don't think so.

PETER: It doesn't take forever to see into somebody.

TORLIEF: I don't see in you.

PETER: Yeah, ya do. Maybe I should freeze you, too. Keep you under ice.

TORLIEF: No.

PETER: Maybe you should freeze me.

TORLIEF: I'm leaving.

PETER: But I know.

TORLIEF: What do you know? What do you know?! What do you know?!?

PETER: You're in hell. You're way down deep in hell. You and me are two damned souls drowning in the lava of hell. It's a collapse from all sides. Everything is going down, pushing it all straight through. Down down down into the lava below. Duck and cover, buddy. Only way to survive. Duck and cover. Get with your buddies. Duck and cover, duck and cover, duck and cover, duck and cover.

(A beat. PETER *stares at his empty stein.* TORLIEF *returns to his chair. Lights fade to black.)*

Scene 10

(Lights up the living room in Mesilla. SCOTT *and* MARGARET *each have turkey sandwiches on paper plates resting in their laps.* SCOTT *listens on a cell phone, then hangs up the phone and puts it in his pants pocket.)*

MARGARET: Why didn't you leave a message for her? You should have left a message that you were checking in.

SCOTT: I'm sure there's nothing wrong.

MARGARET: But your baby daughter.

SCOTT: Theresa would have called if there had been a problem.

MARGARET: You don't know that.

SCOTT: Theresa would have called.

MARGARET: You've been here awhile.

SCOTT: I know that.

MARGARET: What if your daughter is choking?

SCOTT: She's not choking.

MARGARET: What if she is?

SCOTT: That's not happening.

MARGARET: What if your baby daughter is wheezing, her air passage blocked?

SCOTT: Stop.

MARGARET: What if her eyes are rolling back into her head, her mouth hanging open, her arms and legs going limp—

SCOTT: Margaret—

MARGARET: Her chest stops circulating air, her cheeks fall inward, her lips blacken, her heart dries, her bones shatter to dust—

SCOTT: I need to say something, I can't—I need to talk straight with you for a moment. We don't know each other that well and I know you're upset and I understand that you're feeling something bad with the things I've told you. But you shouldn't treat me—you've really no right to talk like that about my daughter in that way even if you're angry and you feel I've done things wrong, that things are wrong, that I've not spoken, that I haven't done things right and I know I haven't done this right but if I'm gonna sit with you here a minute more, you can't talk to me like that. You've got to be nicer than that.

MARGARET: No.

SCOTT: No?

MARGARET: I'm not going to be nicer.

SCOTT: You're not?

MARGARET: No. (Beat) I think you're a disappointment.

SCOTT: I'm a disappointment?

MARGARET: Yes.

SCOTT: How?

MARGARET: What you did.

SCOTT: Okay.

MARGARET: And now.

SCOTT: Now?

MARGARET: You did it. It's changed.

SCOTT: What's changed?

MARGARET: You changed how things were before you told me.

SCOTT: I didn't change things.

MARGARET: You don't see.

SCOTT: What don't I see?

MARGARET: Mike is dead.

SCOTT: Yes.

MARGARET: Before he was dead. And he's still dead. But now its different.

SCOTT: It isn't different.

MARGARET: Mike's dead. *(Beat)* I don't know where this is.

SCOTT: This is this.

MARGARET: I don't know where this is.

SCOTT: It's all right.

MARGARET: It's changed, it's different.

SCOTT: It's all right, it's all right.

MARGARET: Catch me—

(MARGARET *falls.* SCOTT *rushes to catch her. They hold each other.)*

SCOTT: It's all right, it's all right—

(MARGARET *and* SCOTT *sit on the floor. A long pause.)*

SCOTT: The downstairs bathroom drain.

MARGARET: What?

SCOTT: The downstairs bathroom drain at my new house leaked when we first moved in. The pipe under the sink leaked. I had a guy fix it. We'd just moved in. I didn't want to screw up anything. I'm handy with some things but I also know what to leave to the experts. I knew a guy from school who was a plumber, so I called him. He did a good job.

(A pause. MARGARET *begins to stand.)*

MARGARET: A person like that could flood your new house.

SCOTT: Yes.

MARGARET: He could drive you out of your house with this poor plumbing skills.

SCOTT: He could.

MARGARET: He could ruin your home to the point where it is unlivable.

SCOTT: You're right.

*(*SCOTT *leads* MARGARET *to the couch.)*

MARGARET: And you have a new baby. A new baby will cry and sometimes you have no idea why it's crying. If the baby is home crying you should know why. You should look into her eyes and see what it is that hurts. You should look deep, see far, seek and seek. Know what it all is so you don't end up holding your head, wondering what, wondering what. You have to find out what the crying is for.

(A pause)

SCOTT: Eat some sandwich.

MARGARET: I'm not hungry. *(sits)* The world is sinking and churning below me. I can't look. I'm shutting my eyes, I'm shutting my eyes. I can't look.

*(*MARGARET *shuts her eyes.)*

SCOTT: Keep your eyes open. Have a bite of sandwich.

MARGARET: No.

SCOTT: Open your eyes. It's all right.

MARGARET: I can't.

SCOTT: Eat a just a bite.

(SCOTT picks up MARGARET's sandwich. MARGARET opens her eyes and looks at SCOTT.)

SCOTT: Open up.

(A pause. MARGARET opens her mouth. SCOTT tears off a pice of the sandwich and places it near MARGARET's mouth. MARGARET bites the sandwich and chews. A pause. Lights fade to black.)

Scene 11

(Lights up on the makeshift barracks. RAT and GOSS, both quite drunk, sit on their bunks.)

GOSS: If there were guys, guys like in the Universe series, guys that'd come in, freeze something with their goddamn eyes or tear a hole in the ground with their fists, or maybe the "Time Men" or Professor Giddrey Jacobs would show up or Hearthunter even but with Hearthunter then you'd get a whole 'nuther bunch of problems 'cause with Hearthunter comes the world of Hearthunter and then you've got the ice and the cold, the buildings under a mile of frozen seawater so how's that gonna help anything but maybe make it different, a new batch of problems for the Hearthunter to sort through. At least, though, Hearthunter would be there, he'd be around. *(Beat)* Did you know Hearthunter eventually only killed other Hearthunters and stopped killing humans because he felt bad about killing the innocent?

RAT: I hate you.

(A beat)

GOSS: All right.

RAT: Nobody's comin' to save your sorry ass, Gossimer.

GOSS: That's not what I was sayin' at all.

RAT: Yeah you were.

GOSS: The shit just makes sense. *(Pause)* It's just I like comics.

RAT: As a person?

GOSS: "As a person?"

RAT: I'm askin' about you as a person.

GOSS: How are you askin' me that?

RAT: Let's talk.

GOSS: We were doin' that already.

RAT: Let's have a regular conversation.

GOSS: You want some personal shit?

RAT: No. Like—when did you start reading comic books?

GOSS: That's personal.

RAT: Jesus, I'm not askin' if you fucked your dad, I'm only askin' when you started likin' comic books.

GOSS: Rude bastard.

RAT: Spit it out.

(A pause)

GOSS: Since when I was a little kid.

RAT: You liked comics since you were a kid.

GOSS: Yeah.

RAT: How old?

GOSS: Seven or eight or nine.

RAT: What did you like about 'em?

GOSS: The stories.

RAT: When was your first?

GOSS: The hair cut salon my mom went to.

RAT: What was it?

GOSS: *Dark Cloud.*

RAT: *Dark Cloud?*

GOSS: Some shitty little cheap Comicland Adventure comic that musta been there for ten years. It was all ripped up. But I'd look at it every time I was with her down there.

RAT: So you liked the stories?

GOSS: I said that already. Yeah.

RAT: What makes you keep readin' them?

GOSS: What makes me?

RAT: Yeah.

GOSS: Don't know. It's what I do.

RAT: It's what you do.

GOSS: It's me. I read comics.

RAT: You read comics because you're the guy who reads comics?

GOSS: Yeah.

RAT: Shit.

GOSS: Somebody's gotta read 'em and one of those somebody's is me. *(Pause)* What about you?

RAT: What about me?

GOSS: What personal shit you gonna contribute?

RAT: You didn't contribute anythin' much personal.

GOSS: Yeah I did.

RAT: Don't think so.

GOSS: Your turn.

RAT: To do what?

GOSS: Conversation is a two-way street.

RAT: We ain't in couple's therapy, sweetheart.

GOSS: Kiss my ass.

RAT: Not the best way to keep conversation flowing.

(A beat)

GOSS: Where you from, again? You told me once before but I always forget the shit you say.

RAT: Then why repeat it?

GOSS: For purposes of conversation.

(A beat)

RAT: Lindenhurst, Illinois.

GOSS: Where the hell's that again?

RAT: Outside Chicago about forty-five minutes north.

GOSS: What the hell's in Lindenburger, Illinois?

RAT: Houses.

GOSS: Wow.

RAT: Cars.

GOSS: Wow.

RAT: Streets.

GOSS: Damn.

RAT: Outlet mall.

GOSS: Outlet mall.

RAT: Outlet mall.

GOSS: You the shit, Ratto

RAT: You know it.

GOSS: You the biggest shit around. I'm impressed up to my asshole.

RAT: Where you from again? I forget, too.

GOSS: You know where I'm from.

RAT: Under some twenty-pound rock, right?

GOSS: New Mexico. Mesilla, New Mexico.

RAT: Mesilla, with two "L's?"

GOSS: Yeah. "Mes-see-ah," like Mexicans would say.

RAT: Mesilla, New Mexico.

GOSS: Right.

RAT: You able to get good comics in Mesilla, New Mexico?

GOSS: Internet, dumbass.

RAT: What's the best thing in Mesilla, New Mexico?

GOSS: The best thing?

RAT: You drive around, you see something and you say, "Shit, that's the best thing in town." What's that thing?

GOSS: I ain't tellin' you.

RAT: Tell me your favorite goddamn thing in Mesilla goddamn New Mexico or I'll fucking rip out your insides.

(A pause)

GOSS: San Albino Church.

RAT: No shit?

GOSS: Yeah.

RAT: For sure?

GOSS: Yeah.

RAT: Why?

GOSS: It's old.

RAT: Why's it the best thing in town?

GOSS: Cuz it's old.

RAT: How old?

GOSS: Damn old, bro. Real damn fuckin' old. Old.

RAT: Jesus.

GOSS: Plus my horse, that's there, too, and my horse, he's very excellent.

(A pause)

RAT: Beep.

GOSS: What?

RAT: Beep. Outa tape.

GOSS: What?

RAT: Conversation concluded.

GOSS: Concluded?

RAT: Beep.

GOSS: Fucker. I knew you'd act like a dick.

RAT: I'm just being honest with ya.

GOSS: Honest?

RAT: Honest enough to say let's not talk ever again, anymore. Screw your "old" fucking church and screw your goddman "excellent" horse. Let's just be quiet little mice for the rest of our lives here together.

GOSS: Quiet mice?

RAT: Yes.

GOSS: That right?

RAT: Yes.

GOSS: Fuck you.

RAT: Every goddamn thing you say is dumb. It's a pile of uninteresting bullshit and I'm tired of hearing it come out of you.

GOSS: That right?

RAT: Hell yes. This place is a piss-hole and you're the biggest piss in it.

GOSS: Got that wrong.

RAT: No, I got that right.

GOSS: No. You got it wrong.

(RAT *throws his cup at* GOSS.)

RAT: Poison.

GOSS: What you talkin' about?

RAT: Cup full of goddamn poison.

GOSS: I didn't see you spittin' it out.

RAT: Goddamn bullshit sitting here.

GOSS: You got a problem?

RAT: Poison alla this.

GOSS: Who?

RAT: Everything!

GOSS: I ain't done nuthin' to you so go fuck yerself.

RAT: You and your dumb-ass face and your dumb-ass talk and everything around here, its poison.

GOSS: Too bad you ain't goin' noplace, ya hump.

RAT: No place to go if I had someplace to go I'd still end up no place.

GOSS: How you end up here in the first place, jesus.

RAT: It was magic. I was under a magic spell.

GOSS: Funny.

RAT: It was a magic spell put me here. I was in a trance and now I'm here.

GOSS: Snapped outa it now, ain't you.

RAT: Those kids in the car, nonsense with that, and damn shit in here, with you, shit all over the goddamn place, but nuthin' different, huh? Set on fuckin' repeat, all of this.

GOSS: New war is old war.

RAT: What?

GOSS: New war is old war, if that's what you're sayin'—

RAT: Is what what I'm sayin'?

GOSS: New war's the same as old war.

RAT: Where'd you get that?

GOSS: General observation.

RAT: That's not observation. That's cliché.

GOSS: Truth and cliché equals the same bullshit to me.

RAT: I'm caught, then, ain't I?

GOSS: Sure, okay, yeah. You're "caught."

RAT: Caught with you—

(RAT *knocks* GOSS *to the floor and pins him down.*)

RAT: Caught with you, you damn cardboard cutout franchise motherfucker with a gun and a handful of sand in his asscrack. Cliché has slaughtered truth, you numb-nuts bag of shit, so soldier-on, through hill and dale and down the dusty trail. Soldier on.

GOSS: Shut-up like you said you was gonna do already.

RAT: Changed my mind. I think I'm gonna talk instead. It's my turn to tell you some personal shit.

GOSS: I'm gonna go find Hillson.

RAT: Yeah, let Tex regale you with his goddamn pregnant wife stories, cliché, cliché.

GOSS: I gave you half my goddamn haji, dickwad.

RAT: Poison trash.

GOSS: Wasn't.

RAT: Poison poison poison poison!

GOSS: Ain't poison.

RAT: It was POISON! I'VE BEEN FUCKING POISONED! EVERYBODY EVERYWHERE HAS FUCKING POISONED ME TO DEATH! I'm sinking into poison.

(A pause)

GOSS: Nobody talks shit like you do, Ratty.

(RAT pulls his pistol. Standing, RAT aims the pistol at GOSS's chest.)

RAT: You're the one who talks shit. You're the one who talks like he's always exhaling, words and thoughts and everything blows out of your mouth like so much dead breath. You're the one who's exhaling.

(RAT and GOSS breathe. A long pause. RAT silently shoots GOSS in the chest. Lights fade to black.)

Scene 12

(Lights up on the bar in Berlin. PETER and TORLIEF lean heavily on the bar in front of them.)

TORLIEF: Through the desert. Through the Petrified Forest.

PETER: That the place with the trees turned to rock?

TORLIEF: Yeah. Took forever to get there.

PETER: My dad, those long trips, crowned himself the king of the goddamn road.

TORLIEF: Mine, too.

PETER: He'd drive that 1950 Chevy Suburban, pack us kids in—

TORLIEF: Big 'ole Suburban—

PETER: Goddamn air freighter, the original family wagon—

TORLIEF: Wish we had that with ours, kids don't remember cars that way anymore I don't

think—

PETER: Icons of the road, those beasts.

TORLIEF: We did take those trips, though, early on with Mike—

PETER: Took us four days, hit southern Colorado, go up in what was left of those pueblos, crawl through the tunnels, climb the wood ladders.

TORLIEF: Did all that, too, did it with Mike and Margaret—

PETER: Nobody had an answer. Nobody knew what happened, where those people who built those places went.

TORLIEF: Still find pieces of pottery on my property every once in awhile. Shards, arrowheads, broken other things.

PETER: Where did those ones go?

TORLIEF: Not the same people.

PETER: But people none the less.

TORLIEF: They moved on to something else.

PETER: Dwindled away.

TORLIEF: It's a balance, the entirety of it.

PETER: The earth and what it lets survive. A shifting balance, one side to the other.

TORLIEF: Never equal, the balance, is it?

PETER: It's not.

TORLIEF: Some side is always pulling, then the other side pulls but nothing equal exactly.

PETER: Makes sense.

TORLIEF: Makes sense to me.

PETER: So the shards and arrowheads, do you hang on to them?

TORLIEF: Don't find 'em as much as I used to. Mike and me would go out when he was ten or eleven and dig through the dust, look by piles of rocks, see if we could see traces or find an artifact or two.

PETER: That's good fun, digging around, searching for what was there.

TORLIEF: He thought it was a treasure hunt.

PETER: It was.

TORLIEF: It was, you're right.

PETER: Did he keep a collection?

TORLIEF: Yeah.

PETER: In his room?

TORLIEF: Yeah.

PETER: All-American shit, that kinda thing. Don't find kids anywhere else in the world go around in leisure and pick up arrowheads and pottery shards up off the ground and display them in grand fashion.

TORLIEF: I remember something.

PETER: What's that you remember?

TORLIEF: I remember an Indian tribe, an early tribe, a nomadic tribe—the Mansos. They would come through the Mesilla Valley. And the Apache and even Coronado looking for his cities of gold, he went through. And later, Billy the Kid—he was tried and sentenced to hang at the courthouse.

PETER: Wild west.

TORLIEF: Yeah.

PETER: Goddamn wild west America. *(Pause)* Time to go.

TORLIEF: Yeah.

PETER: We'll talk again tomorrow.

TORLIEF: all right.

PETER: You come by here, I'll be right here, and we'll talk.

TORLIEF: Okay.

PETER: Okay.

TORLIEF: See you tomorrow.

PETER: See you tomorrow.

(TORLIEF *stands to exit. He is wobbly on his feet.* PETER *puts a hand on* TORLIEF'*s shoulder.* TORLIEF *stops and looks at* PETER.)

(A pause)

PETER: Once the sun has appeared on the horizon, then all that's passed is gone. Once the moon is at its zenith, then life will start to form. Once the storms rush the sea and the wind whips the fields; once the rain beats the land and the snow covers the peaks; once the fire takes the forest and the smoke chokes the vales—then all that has happened will have happened and all that is new will come once more and begin again—but maybe this time could be without the heavy dose of absolute and numbing bullshit. But I doubt it.

(A pause)

TORLIEF: Goodbye.

PETER: Bye.

(A beat. TORLIEF *and* PETER *shake hands.)*

TORLIEF: Thanks.

PETER: Yeah.

TORLIEF: Bye.

*(*TORLIEF *grabs his coat from a hook and begins to exit.)*

PETER: See you never.

*(*PETER *leans on the bar. Lights fade to black.)*

Scene 13

(Lights up on the living room in Mesilla. SCOTT *and* MARGARET *sit. A long pause as* MARGARET *stares at* SCOTT.*)*

SCOTT: Mike told me that The Hearthunter, he had a sidekick. The sidekick was not infected as most humans were, he was just a skinny little former businessman, but the man had an artificial heart so The Hearthunter didn't desire to rip open his chest. The Hearthunter kept the man around as some kind of comic relief or more likely to have some perspective on what was left after the new ice age and disease had torn apart the world. Mike also told me The Hearthunter would walk the earth along an ice bridge that formed in the northern region and he'd seek out answers or possibly a cure for what had happened to humanity, possibly a way to return his own self to the man he was before, return himself to the man who had once lived a common life, to the man who once knew nothing of hardship or famine or the desperate need to survive without losing ones mind.

MARGARET: An unhappy existence.

SCOTT: Not unhappy, I don't think, but *heroic*. Heroic, given the kind of difficult future that lay ahead.

(A beat)

MARGARET: Goodbye.

SCOTT: Bye.

MARGARET: Goodbye.

(SCOTT *exits.* MARGARET *sits on the couch. She picks up the phone and holds it. Lights fade to black.)*

END OF PLAY

www.ingramcontent.com/pod-product-compliance
Lightning Source LLC
Chambersburg PA
CBHW070025110426
42741CB00034B/2604